Anne-Katrin Hagen

Rider's Aids

CADMOS
EQUESTRIAN

Contents

Imprint

Copyright of this edition © 2004 by Cadmos
Copyright of original edition © 2003 by Cadmos
Verlag GmbH, Brunsbek
Project management: Editmaster Co Ltd.
Translated by: Claire Williams
Design and setting: Ravenstein, Verden
Printed by: Grindel Druck, Hamburg
All rights reserved
Copying or storage in electronic media is per-
mitted only with the prior written permission of
the publishers.
Printed in Germany

ISBN 3-86127-942-8

What type of creature is the horse?

Riding is another word for communicating with your horse: you make it clear to your horse what he should do, and when all goes according to plan he does it. And in addition no one should see what you did to get him to do it. This involves the precise application of aids and this equates to good riding.

Note

Even if you love your horse, avoid treating him as a person. A horse is a horse and thinks and behaves like one.

Note

The horse originated on the plains and is a herd animal of flight.

To be fair to such an animal, it must be given the opportunity to move freely. Ride daily and turn out as much as possible. A horse's instinct to run away is expressed in different degrees of intensity in today's horses. It does no good whatsoever to punish a horse that spooks easily or seizes any chance to take off. You would in fact achieve the opposite. The only course of action is for the rider to build up trust with the horse.

If you want to win over a herd animal, you must take over the role of leader. That means you must earn the horse's respect in all situations. If your horse gets stroppy when being tacked up, fidgets when being groomed, barges when being led – all must be consistently stopped as they threaten your position as herd leader. Clear commands such as "Stand up" "Halt" or "Hoof", supported by clear signals, all help to exert authority. A tug on the head col-

To make yourself understood by your horse the riding aids are applied to his receptive zones:
* The mouth for the aids from the rein or hand. These aids work through the poll, neck and back though to the hindquarters.
* The sides of the neck and the withers for praise, reassurance and scratching.
* The back for the seat and weight aids.
* The arch of the ribs on both sides for the leg aids.

The horse's receptive zones

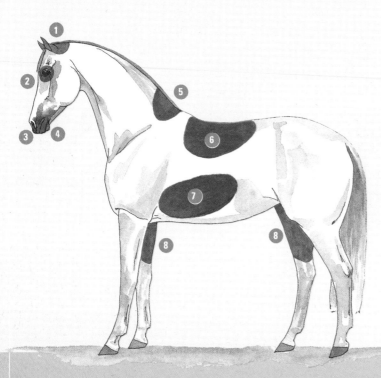

1. *They hear everything! But best of all prais
and reassurance.*
2. *They are not sharp sighted, but can see
light, shadows and movements (especially
of monsters) precisely.*
3. *Distinguishes between good and bad plan
and indicates "I like you" or "I don't like
you".*
4. *Is very sensitive and should not be
mistreated by rough hands!*
5. *The preferred area for praise and stroking*
6. *The many nerves and muscles here sense
the distribution of the rider's weight.*
7. *Here the horse is receptive to the rider's I*
8. *In these places the horse's skin is very th
No dried sweat or sand should be left her
to rub*

The seat and leg aids are central to riding. These aids should flow from the hindquarters over the back up the neck, over the poll and down to the mouth along the length of the horse from back to front. It is possible to strengthen the leg temporarily with the use of spurs and touch the hind legs gently with a whip to make it more active. The voice is used to calm, praise and when necessary occasionally caution. All of these opportunities to make yourself understood by your horse through correct use of the natural and artificial aids assume that the rider is in the right position.

Note

Good riding begins with grooming as the entire coat and the skin underneath are very sensitive. Just watch what happens when a fly lands on a horse.

The dressage position

There are three different positions or seats: the dressage or normal seat; the forward or jumping seat, and the jockey seat. Since the last one is only used on the racetrack or by riders in three-day events, we will not touch any further on this one.

Note

The correct position is the foundation for good riding, regardless of the discipline.

If a rider sits in this natural and relaxed way in the saddle, it should be possible to draw a vertical line from the ear through the shoulder and hip down to the ankle.

What does the correct position look like?

In the dressage seat you should sit deep in the saddle evenly balanced on both seat bones and let your legs hang down loosely. The balls of the feet should rest on the stirrups. The heel should be the lowest point of the rider, with the feet parallel to the horse so that the calf (and not the heel) lies flat against the horse's body. If you are wearing spurs you can be sure that your leg position is correct if the spurs are positioned to the rear and down, and not unintentionally digging the horse in his ribs. When the heel is down and the calf is flat against the horse, the ankle will be able to absorb movement up and down the leg. This is vital.

The upper body should be straight without being tense and the head should be held up, looking forwards through the horse's ears. The shoulders should be moved slightly up and back and then relaxed down. The arms should hang naturally by the side. Then gently close the fists (with the thumbs lying on top) and bend the arms at the elbows until the fists are about a hand's width from the withers. This gives the correct arm and hand positioning.

The forearm and reins should form a line by themselves and the correct lower leg position is immediately behind the girth.

Seen from behind, the rider's head and back together with the middle of the horse's croup and his tail form a vertical line, while the shoulders, hips and feet of the rider form three horizontal parallel lines.

Incorrect positions

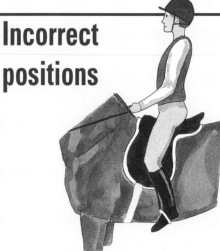

The Forked Seat
Here the rider is not sitting deep in the saddle and spreading the weight over both seat bones. Instead the thighs are taking the weight and the rider is in front of the vertical, making balance impossible. This position is frequently caused by stirrups that are too long or by a saddle whose lowest point is too far forward.

The Armchair Seat
The rider is sitting too far back on the saddle. The knee and thigh are drawn up and the seat muscles are tensed, with the rider behind the vertical. This gives the rider little opportunity to use his seat and he is likely to lose his balance. Usually stirrups that are too short or a saddle whose lowest point is too far back are the cause.

Note

Correct aids can only be applied from a balanced, relaxed seat. A rider's suppleness must never be lost, if she wants to maintain a correct position. No horse can go in a relaxed manner under a tense rider.

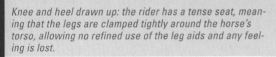

Knee and heel drawn up: the rider has a tense seat, meaning that the legs are clamped tightly around the horse's torso, allowing no refined use of the leg aids and any feeling is lost.

The rider is not looking in the direction that the horse is going. If the rider looks straight ahead while the horse is bending (on a circle or a volte) then the rider is also likely to remain straight through the shoulders. This then loses the parallel line between the horse's and rider's shoulders and hips. As a result the harmony between both will suffer and the horse is likely to lose his balance. If you always look through the horse's ears then you will always automatically follow the correct line to ride.

Crooked seat: The rider is bent through the hip and is putting more weight on the opposite seat bone. The shoulder will usually be pulled up over the weighted hip and drops the other side.

Stiff wrists and rolled hands: rolled over hands are a common problem. The hands are rolled over so the thumbs lie on the side and not on top of the fists. Finer aids cannot be given with the hands like this, as it is only possible to pull with the reins – poor horse. The same applies to wrists that are too tense and stiff – this results in hard hands.

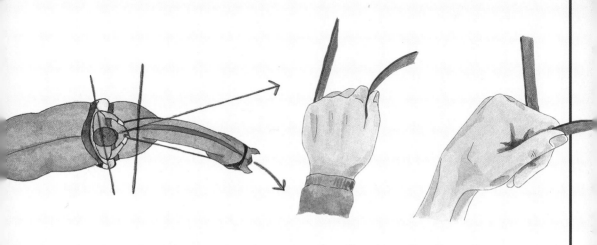

The aids

To make it clear to the horse what you want him to do the rider has what we know as the natural aids at his disposal. These are:

1. The seat – or weight aids – used on both sides, one sided or not used at all.
2. The legs, that can be used to create forwards movement, forwards sideways m o v e - ment or used to support.
3. Hands that can give, take, hold, block, support and direct.

Only when the aids are working in harmony and applied by a rider with a correct, supple and balanced seat is harmony between horse and rider at all paces possible. In principle the aids encouraging forwards movement (seat and legs) are more important than the restrainung aids (rein or hand).

for example when cantering and as a prerequisite for a change of direction.

If, for example, you want the horse to turn to the right, the right seat bone should be pushed forwards and downwards while the hips remain braced. Your torso should always be stretched tall and avoid collapsing through the hip. This aid is also a prerequisite for leg and rein aids.

A *lighter* seat is used when the horse's back and hindquarters need to be relieved of weight, allowing the horse to move more freely. The seat remains in the saddle but the weight moves more onto the thigh and knee, while the upper body leans slightly forward. This aid is useful when training young horses, warming up, riding up gentle slopes and for the first attempts at reining back.

The seat

When used simultaneously *on both sides* the legs should lie on the girth line. Both seat bones will be exerting pressure forwards and downwards towards the knee and heel. The upper body stays upright and the stomach muscles are tightened. This is called "bracing the back". This isn't a constant aid, but rather is used just for a moment. Bracing the back is a signal for the horse's hindquarters to become more active. If used with a giving hand the horse should trot on.

A *one-sided* aid from the seat is used when the horse is flexed or positioned to the inside,

The rider should shift his weight in the direction of the horse's mouth – i.e. forwards and down

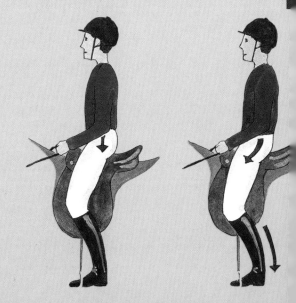

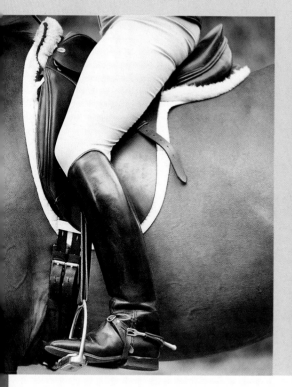

The forwards driving leg on the girth.

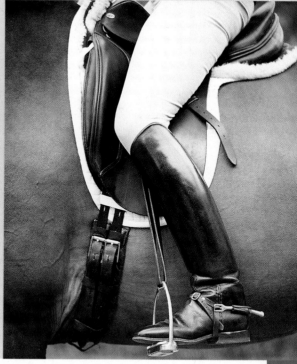

The forwards-sideways driving leg a hand's breadth behind the girth.

The legs

The *forwards* driving leg aid drives the horse forward in all paces, with the rider's leg just behind the girth applying a gentle pressure on both sides.

The *forwards-sideways driving* leg aid is used in lateral work, including leg yielding, whereby the rider's lower leg lies a hand's breadth behind the girth. The knee and heel should not be drawn up. The forwards-sideways leg aid supports the one-sided engagement of the rider's seat.

The *supporting leg aid* is used as a balance opposite the forwards or forwards-sideways driving aid by preventing the hindquarters from falling out. The supporting leg, like the sideways driving aid is also placed about a hand's breadth behind the girth but is not as active.

The hands

The hands should never be used in isolation. Only a horse that is working through allows the aids from the hands to work from the mouth over the poll, down the neck and back into the hindquarters. The horse lets the aids through, in other words he accepts the hand and is submissive to the aid.

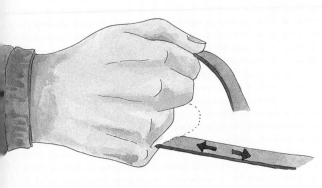

Active and yielding rein aids are short impulses, made without tugging or clinging.

ward. The pressure that results from this must be held until the horse gives in to the rider, accepts the bit and becomes lighter in the hand. This moment must not be missed, as the hands must immediately become softer and the seat relaxed as a reward to the horse! This way the horse will better understand what we want from him.

Directional rein aids are used when the horse is to move along a curved line, for example a circle. On the left rein, the left hand is moved across inwards very slightly so that the horse's left eye and nostril are just visible. On the right hand of course the opposite happens. The directional aid is always given with the *supporting* aid that helps to maintain the curve. Thus on the left rein the supporting rein would be the right hand. These aids are always given with the one-sided active leg aid and the one-sided weight aid. The inside leg is therefore pushing to the outside hand. Together with the one-sided engagement of the seat this makes a diagonal aid, and is the prerequisite for many exercises.

A *sideways leading* rein aid will particularly help young horses in the direction of the bend. This is also useful when teaching lateral movements. Accompanied by the relevant weight aid, the hand is moved away from the horse's neck and over slightly in the direction of the intended movement. Once the horse has accepted this aid, the other hand should give to follow the active hand.

With the *active* (erroneously called "taking") rein aid the hand is closed more firmly or slightly turned to the inside in order to shorten the rein a little – in both cases only for a moment. This is not possible if you have rolled your hands over; pulling on the reins is the greatest sin!

An active hand is always followed by a *yielding* hand. The hands return to their usual position with relaxed fingers around the reins. This does not mean that the contact to the horse's mouth should be broken; it should always be there even with the yielding rein aid.

Blocking rein aids are used when the horse goes against the hand or above the reins. The hands are in their usual position, the back is braced and the legs are actively driving for-

On a long rein the horse stretches forwards and down. The rider should still maintain a contact with the horse's mouth.

On a completely loose rein the rider lets the reins out to the buckle. There is no contact with the horse's mouth and the horse has a lowered head and neck.

Note

The hand should never to be used in isolation. The hand alone cannot force the horse to give at the poll. A horse that works on a regular and constant contact with the rider's hands with a relaxed jaw is said to be on the bit.

Artificial aids

The voice is vital to win your horse's trust. The voice can be used to calm young horses, but only when it is also used in the stable or when grooming. If a young horse isn't familiar with the human voice, then it is of little use when you try to use it in an emergency. The voice can also be used to encourage or discipline. When a young horse is more advanced in his training then he should be able to be worked without using the voice. It should, however, always be used to praise. In competition such as a dressage test your horse should be the only one to hear it, though! Thank goodness that horses have such sharp hearing.

A *whip* should be used to get a horse's attention. In dressage a light touch on the hind legs can increase the engagement. Careless use or constant tickling with a whip can make a horse rushed or anxious, or can lead to a horse ignoring it entirely. The whip is usually carried by the inside hand so that it can activate the inside hind leg. At every change of rein, the whip should also change hands.

A slap with a jumping whip means "Come on – move on!" Jumping whips should never be carried with the grip at the bottom, i.e. upside down. This is both dangerous and unprofessional. A dressage whip may not be longer than 1.2 metres and a jumping whip should never be more than 75cm over its entire length.

You need to earn your *spurs* – meaning only those with a quiet leg and an independent seat should wear spurs. Spurs emphasise the aids from the leg and should be used precisely and briefly, not constantly dug into a horse's side. This will hurt your horse and can deaden him to the aid. The point of the spur should always be shaped such that it cannot hurt the horse. For horses it should not be longer than 4.5cm and for ponies 3.5cm long.

Now all of the aids have been discussed individually in theory. The difficulty in riding is that many aids need to work together at one time. How strongly each of the aids needs to be given depends on the situation and the individual horse. This demands a great deal of feeling and experience from the rider that can only be learnt in time.

Basic training

Halts and half-halts

The halt

A rider needs to learn about the halt at an early stage so she can stop her horse. The halt is only asked for on a straight line and can occur from any pace, although when starting out it should only be done from the walk and trot. A strong half-halt always leads to a halt! A more active seat and legs push the horse into a blocking hand that yields to become soft just before the horse comes to a halt. Horses use their necks as a counterbalance to come to a calm and square halt. Stepping back and forth, not standing square, and head nodding, are all considered major faults. The latter indicates a heavy hand.

This shows the correct application of the aids to halt.

A half-halt is not a single action but instead is applied in rhythm with the movement. It is used:

• To make transitions from one pace to an-other
• To regulate the tempo within a pace
• To prepare the horse for some sort of change, for example of pace, movement, etc.
• To create, keep and improve the contact and later to collect the horse
• Overall, to ride the horse correctly.

Here the rider is just pulling on the reins — please don't try to halt like this!

Half-halt

More important but also harder to use is the half-halt. All aids (leg, seat and hands) are used at the same time for the half-halt. The rider puts more weight into the seat, braces the back, closes the leg and restricts the horse from tak-ing off in front with a restraining hand. The rider is in effect pushing the horse together from the back to the front and immediately follows with a giv-ing hand or rein.

The half-halt is a brief impulse given simultaneously from the legs, seat and hands.

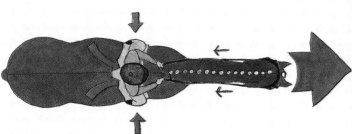

The walk is a four-beat pace with no impulsion.

Riding the basic paces correctly

Walk

Once you are in the saddle, you need to check your position from the seat bones and hips up to head, arms and hands, and then down to the tips of the toes, bit by bit as if going through a checklist. Tip the pelvis forwards from a braced back – you should notice the pressure on both seat bones. Both calves should lie actively against the girth and the hands should move slightly forwards. This all needs to happen at the same time and will work as a signal to tell the horse to move forwards – hopefully caus-ing the horse to walk on! The walk has four beats and should be purposeful but calm. In the walk we talk about steps, and the horse will move his head up and down slightly so it is important that the rider's hands follow the horse's movement, otherwise the horse will come up against the bit at every stride.

Trot

To trot on, repeat the aids from the halt into walk. The trot has two beats. In a working trot the strides should be regular, covering the ground with impulsion. The trot is the hardest of the three paces to sit to comfortably because the horse's back swings in a strong forwards up and

The trot is a two-beat pace with impulsion.

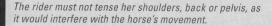

The rider must not tense her shoulders, back or pelvis, as it would interfere with the horse's movement.

This shows the movement of a horse when the rider tenses his back.

In trot the horse moves in a forwards flowing movement.

down movement. The rider's back needs to match this swinging movement so that the seat doesn't bang down into the saddle, but instead sticks to it like glue. You should sit with relaxed seat muscles and a naturally straight back in the deepest part of the saddle. You should in effect become part of the horse. Only the legs should urge the horse on forwards and should lie quietly on the girth with a light pressure. It is all too easy for the rider to tense up – the shoulders get pulled up, the chin pokes out or the head nods in time to the movement.

Tensing up the upper body and clamping the legs around the horse are just as bad (as well as being harmful to the horse) as too soft a back (like a wobbly jelly) or a leg banging against the side of the horse in time to the movement. It is easy to see therefore that the rider has to prac-

tise many different exercises until capable of using well-directed aids in the trot with finesse. Despite the amount of movement in trot the hands need to remain quiet, with the up and down movement absorbed through the elbow. Imagine that you are holding a glass of water in each hand: in the trot you should not spill a single drop of water. This is only possible when the shoulders and wrist remain relaxed.

Rising trot

Once your seat is secure it is possible to make your horse's life easier through rising trot. First look at your horse's shoulder and observe how they move back and forth. Then count along in time – one-two, one-two, one-two. One is the outside, two is the inside shoulder. In time with two, rise up from the knee and with one go back down into the saddle – but don't thud back down! The knees should be held firmly against the saddle and the lower legs should remain quiet with the heels down.

The upper body should remain upright (only in a forward seat should you tilt forward slightly) and when you sit back down in the saddle the pelvis should be tilted slightly forward and together with both legs pushes the horse forwards. The hands should be held very still with

The movement into a rising trot should come from the knee.

Here the rider is pulling himself up on the reins. There is no obvious sign of moving with the horse!

the elbows acting to absorb the movement, which in rising trot is stronger because the rider too is moving up and down. If you ask your horse to change the rein then you as the rider also have to change rein. If for example you're changing the rein across the school in rising trot (from the left to the right rein), ride across the diagonal on the left rein and one horse's length before reaching the long side stay sitting for two strides before rising again. You should count: 1-2, 1-2, 1-1-2.

You should now be trotting on the left (outside) foreleg and the right (inside) hind leg. When you've mastered rising trot you will find it the best way of covering longer distances. Remember though to change from the left to right rein when hacking out – even if you are riding in straight lines.

The canter is a three-beat gait.

The canter

The canter is a three-beat gait that, due to its roundness and impulsion, is much easier to sit to than the trot. It is easy to count along when the canter is a good one (something to watch out for): one- two-three, one-two-three. If you can count one-twohoo-three, one-twohoo-three, then the clear three-beat rhythm has been lost to become a four-beat canter. This is a major fault and the only thing that helps is to ride strongly forwards. It also pays to check that the contact is giving enough. Left and right canter are distinguished by whether it is the right or left foreleg that reaches further forward. If you are on the left rein you would normally be on the left canter lead.

For the beginner (almost all new riders look forward to their first canter), it is easiest to canter for the first time by riding in sitting trot on the left rein. On the open circle side lower the outside right hand while taking a slightly firmer contact and at the same time give slightly with the inside left hand. Sometimes it's enough to open the fingers a little. At the same time, weight the inside left seat bone forwards and downwards (one-sided weighted seat aid) and place the right leg a hand's breadth (no more!) behind the girth (supporting leg aid), while the left leg is on the girth driving forwards. As the horse joins the track again push him into canter (the side of the school prevents the horse from rushing if the rider's aids are still not perfect). These aids must all be given at the same time. The right shoulder should not be left behind and the position as described should be maintained through the entire canter.

In canter a horse moves like a rocking horse and the rider needs to balance the movement of the canter strides between the hips and

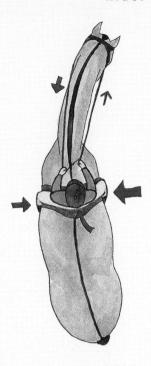

All aids must be applied simultaneously. The strongest pressure comes from the inside leg. For the left canter the opposite applies.

knees into the saddle for the first few trot strides after the transition, so as not to bump around on the horse's back. Whatever you do, don't stand up in the stirrups. Once you have learned to sit out those critical first few strides, try to ensure that those first trot strides are as smooth as the fifth or sixth, to ensure a smoother transition.

The transition from trot to walk is done exactly like that from canter to trot. All these transitions are achieved through cleanly ridden half-halts and should be ridden as often as possible when schooling. They loosen the horse up and when the aids are applied correctly encourage the horse to take up a contact and to pay attention. Transitions within and between paces will also help the rider to develop a better feel.

elbows. The upper body needs to stay upright and quiet, with the legs staying on and behind the girth without moving back and forth. If the rider tips forwards or even bends forwards to check if the horse is on the correct leg, the horse will become unbalanced, as the aids to maintain the canter can then no longer be given. It is enough to just glance down to check if the correct leg is reaching forwards.

If the rider wants to transition back to trot, then both legs should be placed on the girth, she should sit upright, take up a firmer contact (but don't pull!) and sink her weight into the saddle. In doing this the pressure from the calves should be increased and the rider should be thinking in a two- instead of three-beat pace. For the first few times it can help to press the

Flexion and bend

So that our horse doesn't go around corners like a bus, we have to encourage suppleness through the length of the horse. This starts with flexion. *Flexion* means the sideways bending of the horse through his poll with the neck and back remaining straight. Flexion is clearly required when, for example, cantering, turning on the forehand or leg yielding.

Inwards flexion is achieved by weighting both seat bones and giving with the outside rein as much as the inside one is taken. The contact must not be totally given away. Try this out while stationary – flex the horse slowly to the left and then to the right. Only the head should be moved

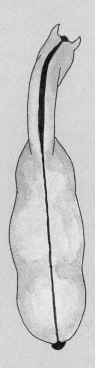

The body of the horse should remain straight when he is flexed inwards.

rect circle, and a greater bend is needed for a volte (ten metre circle and smaller). The smaller the circle's diameter (ten, eight or six metre), the greater the bend needs to be: for many movements the exact bend is essential.

Bend is created by the correct application of diagonal aids. Weight the inside seat bone forwards and downwards while encouraging the inside hind leg through by keeping the inside leg on the girth. The supporting outside leg lies a hand's breadth behind the girth to prevent the quarters falling out. The inside rein positions the head to the inside and leads the horse into the bend, if required. At the same time the outside rein gives as much as needed, depending on the positioning and bend. The outside rein prevents too great a bend and controls the outside shoulder. If the outside rein is too weak or if the horse doesn't work through into the outside rein (usually only the case on one rein), then he will fall out through the shoulder.

To ride curved lines correctly the horse must be straight. He must have learnt to move on straight and curved lines with the fore and hind legs following like a train on tracks.

and then only far enough to see the inside eye and the edge of his nostrils. You should also see the mane tip over at the crest to the side to which the horse's head is pointed. Once you have done this at a halt try it at walk and trot. The flexion will be incorrect if the inside rein is pulled or the outside rein is not given enough and this will be seen by the horse getting too tight through the neck. Too much bend is also wrong. The horse will then fall out through the outside shoulder and his paces will become irregular. If the rider's weight is not evenly distributed over both seat bones the horse will find it impossible to stretch the inside hind leg through and under.

By *bend* we mean the curvature of the horse through his length, from the poll, over the back to his tail. A slight bend is needed to ride a cor-

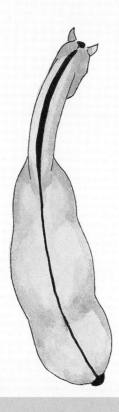

The bend goes through the horse's length

Riding corners

A beginner rider will soon be confronted with corners, although riding a corner correctly is not all that easy. A corner should be ridden like a quarter ten metre circle, although at the start it is flattened out somewhat. The horse must however be bent correctly. Before the corner the rider needs to give one or two half-halts and position the horse to the inside. Using diagonal aids the horse should be sufficiently bent and then once out of the corner should be straightened again. As you may imagine, a correctly ridden circle is a very good exercise for both horse and rider. It requires concentration and elasticity from the horse, and discipline from the rider.

Changing of rein across the diagonal

After the corner keep the horse positioned to the inside and at the next marker (when the horse's nose reaches the letter) turn the horse onto the diagonal. The inside leg and the outside rein will ensure that the horse doesn't turn in too early. Once on the diagonal the horse should be straightened and the rider should look at the point where she intends to join the track, so that the line ridden is straight. A half-halt then precedes the next corner.

Riding circles

When riding on a circle a slight but regular bend is necessary, achieved once again through diagonal aids. On a circle a rider can learn how much inside leg and outside hand is needed for her horse to stay on an even and regular circle. A circle is, as the word suggests,

Note

There is no bend without flexion! On the other hand, flexion without bend is often used, for example, on a turn on the forehand or in leg yielding.

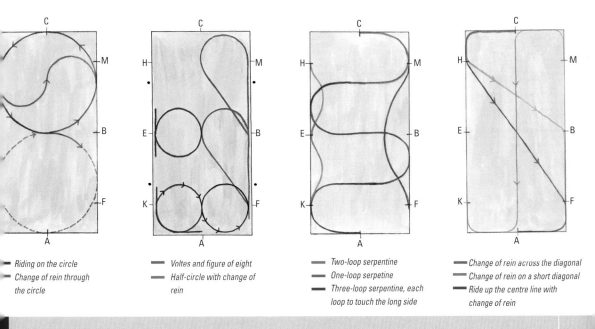

Riding on the circle
Change of rein through
the circle

Voltes and figure of eight
Half-circle with change of
rein

Two-loop serpentine
One-loop serpetine
Three-loop serpentine, each
loop to touch the long side

Change of rein across the diagonal
Change of rein on a short diagonal
Ride up the centre line with
change of rein

Schooling figures

circular. There are no corners and it isn't oval like an egg! It has three points of contact to the track, one of which on the short side coincides with A or C. It is only at these points of the circle that the circle should touch the track. The fourth point is the imaginary point X in the middle of the school. If you have trouble riding a truly round circle, then think of the circle as a square whose corners are the points of the circle. If in a dressage test the command is circle at A, then the curve starts at A and the next corner is missed so that the circle will next touch the track at the point of the circle which lies beyond the corner. Similarly if the command is to go large at A, then a well-ridden corner should follow A.

Changing from one bend to the other

Changing the rein out of the circle, serpentines and figures of eight are exercises that require swift changes in the horse's bend. Before the transition to the new rein the horse should be prepared with a half-halt and straightened for a horse's length. The rider should change himself onto the new rein by sitting out a stride, readjust his reins (judges like to see that!) and clearly ask for the new bend. At the start allow plenty of time, otherwise the horse may be pulled around and that of course is incorrect. The change in bend must be a smooth, fluid movement.

In a volte the aids must be given clearly and carefully

tioned in the direction of the movement. On reaching the marker give another half-halt and apply the diagonal aids – these need to given precisely. If too much inside rein is used the horse will be pulled around; if there isn't enough outside rein given then there will not be enough bend; if the inside leg is not strong enough, rhythm and impulsion will be lost; if the outside leg doesn't provide enough support, the horse's quarters will trail because he will find this easier. Starting from where the circle begins, use both legs and reins to lead the horse around the curve of the circle ending it exactly at the starting point. Riding a good circle is not that easy! Every volte requires care and patience – step-by-step and stride-by-stride. Any haste or carelessness will be immediately obvious.

Voltes

The volte demands the greatest degree of lateral bend from a horse. The hind legs must follow the fore legs exactly on the same track. This is why in preliminary and novice dressage the circles are still relatively large, at ten metres.

Before reaching the point at which the volte should start, the horse's attention should be gained with a half-halt and he should be posi-

Half-circles with a change of reins

Wherever this figure is ridden, the first half is always ridden just like a volte. At the point furthest from the track the horse should be straightened and ridden at an angle straight back to the track. On this straight line both legs and seat bones should be used evenly. It is vital to watch that the horse stays on one track and doesn't drift onto more than one track as if in travers or to drift over as if leg yielding.

Serpentines

Serpentines across the school are usually ridden with three or four loops at first, later though may be ridden with five loops. The serpentine begins and ends in the middle of the short side. In the case of a three-loop serpentine on the right rein beginning at A, a half 10 metre circle is ridden, in effect rounding off the corner before straightening the horse for a bit, then positioning the horse to the inside, shortening the reins slightly, riding the next half-circle to the other rein, touching the track at B. This is followed by another straight line until the next half-circle, which then finishes at C. The next corner should be ridden correctly too. A good serpentine will depend as much on the horse's willingness to change bend and go straight between the circles as the rider's ability to ask the horse to do this correctly.

Serpentines on the long side are a bit more difficult and can be ridden with single or double loops. A single loop serpentine is ridden to a depth of five metres out from the track (i.e. a quarter of the school's width). After correctly riding the corner the horse is bent to the inside and moves away from the track at the marker (i.e. not at the point of the circle). After about two horse lengths the bend is changed so that the outside leg now becomes the inside leg. The furthest point out from the track is reached opposite E/B at five metres from the track and on reaching this point you start to return to the track, again changing the bend about two horse-lengths out from the track, meeting the track at the corner marker so that a correctly ridden corner can follow.

In the two-loop serpentine everything happens a bit faster. The furthest the horse moves away from the track is two and a half metres and in the middle the horse returns to the track at E or B, meaning the changes of bend happen fairly quickly.

The rider must be confident in giving the correct aids – she must be able to give the diagonal and simultaneous aids in quick succession and mustn't forget the half-halts in the process.

The horse must be supple and relaxed. Any stiffness from either horse or rider will be noticed immediately, making this exercise an ideal test of a rider's independent seat and soft hands and the horse's obedience and suppleness.

Note

In turns, especially ten metre circles, the inside rein must never dominate. Otherwise you risk the horse becoming too tense through the poll, he may get behind the vertical and will be pulled around into the circle. It is vital that in circles, the reins should never be used in isolation but should always be supported by the seat and leg aids.

Leg yielding

Leg yielding is a loosening exercise which should help develop a horse's submission and prepare it for the lateral aids. As a result of leg yielding the rider's inside leg pushes the horse more into the outside hand. The horse moves forwards and sideways on two tracks slightly flexed but without bending so that he moves twice as far forwards as he does sideways, with the inside fore and hind feet moving evenly forwards and over the outside feet.

When leg yielding the fore and hind legs move forwards and sideways over the outside pair.

The angle should not be too great. In leg yielding the horse should move forwards.

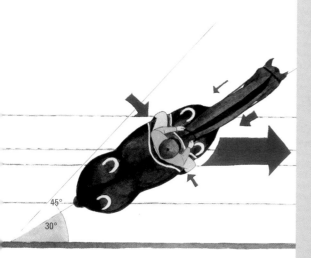

The horse is always flexed to the side of the rider's active, driving leg. The rider needs to put more weight on the inside seat bone, with the inside leg lying just behind the girth and driving forwards and sideways, while the outside leg supports just behind the girth, preventing the hindquarters dropping out and keeping the forward movement. The inside rein creates a slight flexion and the outside rein prevents too great a bend and keeps the shoulder from falling out.

Turn on the forehand

Turn on the forehand is a loosening exercise and is used to get the horse accustomed to the lateral aids. After the aids to halt (in an indoor school this should be on the inside track so that there is room for the horse's head and neck to turn) the horse should be flexed to the outside. The rider should weight the (new) inside seat bone and using her leg positioned slightly back, drives the horse round step by step so that the hindquarters turn around the forehand.

The outside rein (which has just been the inside rein) ensures that there is not too much bend through the neck. The supporting outside leg ensures that the hindquarters don't move round too quickly. Thus the horse is moved away from the leg pushing sideways, the inside hind leg steps in front of and across the outside leg while the outside foreleg steps around the inside fore.

After the 180 degree turn the horse should be positioned in halt again. During the entire movement the rider must watch that the horse

Rein back

It is very important that you can ride a halt from a walk or trot without the horse going against the hand, falling out behind or tossing his head. He should stand square with the weight evenly distributed over all four legs. If this isn't the case and he doesn't give through the poll or he stands crooked with the hindquarters falling out then it will be impossible for him to accept the aids without resistance. In the rein back the horse should move diagonal pairs of legs backwards (foot fall as in trot but without the moment of suspension). He shouldn't drag his feet through the sand but instead should step cleanly back. The rider gives the same aids as for moving off forwards but at the moment in which the horse lifts his leg, the rider shifts her weight a little from the seat bones to the upper thigh and knee. The upper body should not, however, tip forward! Both lower legs should lie against the horse's sides to stop him moving sideways and the rider takes up the rein slightly by turning in the hands. These aids must all happen at the same time so that the forwards impetus is used to move backwards. At the moment when the horse does move back the hand should be lightened without giving up the contact. For the next step the same procedure is followed – thus every step is individually ridden.

Once the required number of steps have been completed (usually three to four) the rein should be given and the rider asks for a square halt, letting the horse stand quietly.

A whole host of things can go wrong when trying to rein back. They happen most frequently when the horse is not standing in halt correctly or when the rider pulls on the reins without giving the horse the forwards momentum with seat

Using sideways active seat and leg aids the rider asks her horse to move around the forehand step by step. The outside leg and the outside rein support throughout.

stays on the bit and moves neither forwards (a minor mistake) nor backwards (a greater error because it shows that the hand has been acting backwards).

When allowing the horse to take the reins down, the rider must ride forwards so that the horse doesn't drop back into trot or walk.

This horse is stepping back regulary on a soft contact.

Here it's all being done wrong.

and legs. The rider may pull in her stomach muscles and pull her heels up so that her upper body tips forwards. No aids can be correctly given like this. When both legs don't support enough, or do so unevenly, then the rein back will be crooked. Hard or unyielding hands will cause the horse to back up too quickly or back up while tossing his head. If a rider remains too heavily in the saddle the horse won't understand what is being asked of him.

Giving and retaking the reins is a fluid move-
ment and should last several seconds.

Allowing the horse to take the reins down

Taking the reins down out of the hand can happen in all paces. At the start it is recommended that it be done from a walk, later at a trot and only when it is safe to do so should this be done at a canter. Riding at a normal working pace the rider should open her fingers slightly and the horse should take the bit forwards and down. The pace should not quicken and balance should not be lost. The horse should stretch softly down until the head reaches the height of the stirrups but he should stay in front of the vertical. The rider's hand should move in the direction of the horse's mouth but should maintain a soft contact. The rider will need to continue to push on because most horses become lazier during this exercise. It is better to practise this exercise frequently for short periods. If the horse goes for too long in this extended outline, there is a risk than he will go too much on the forehand.

Giving and retaking the reins

This exercise is a test of a horse's self-carriage and shows whether he is working securely off his rider's seat and leg aids. The rider pushes both hands forwards along the neck for about two to three strides. The hands are then softly returned to where they started. This exercise can also be done in all paces.

In a forward seat you should be able to draw a vertical line down from the shoulder through the knee to the ball of the foot.

The forward seat

The forward seat is used in many different situations when riding. For this reason the forward seat has a number of forms depending on the position, whether this be jumping seat, jockey seat, cross-country seat or forward seat. In the forward seat the rider lightens her seat, taking her weight of the horse's back, and adapts herself to the movement of the horse, which in general will be stronger than when working on the flat. The forward seat is usually ridden in a general purpose or jumping saddle. As a result of their shape (forward cut and shorter saddle flaps, longer and flatter seat) it is easier to ride in a for-

ward seat correctly. In comparison to a dressage position, the stirrups are noticeably shorter: when riding young horses or when hacking out they are two holes shorter, and when jumping or riding cross-country, four to five holes shorter. The number of holes varies according to the rider's size and length of leg.

In a forward position it is much easier for the rider to adjust to the horse's movement. When the horse's centre of gravity changes, for example when jumping or going up or down hill, and when the speed is increased in gallop, the rider is able to balance with her upper body and adjust her weight appropriately. The transitions within the position should be fluid. Knee, calf, ankle and the foot in the stirrup, i.e. the foundation, remain unaltered throughout.

In a forward seat the upper body will be tipped forwards from the hip, the degree varying according to demand. When the demands are less, the seat remains more in the saddle, while at high speed or when jumping the seat will remain out of the saddle longer. The rider though should always maintain her flexibility through the middle part of her body and the spine should always be in a natural position.

Note

Just as when riding in a dressage position, a stiff or unsteady upper body riding in a forward seat with tensed shoulders, hunched or hollow back is just as incorrect and interferes just as much with the horse.

The knees should lie against the saddle and are bent at a greater angle due to the shorter stirrups. The knees are the critical point when riding in a forward seat. If that contact at the knee is lost then things will get difficult for the rider. The lower leg lies with the calf flat on the girth and thus on the horse – otherwise the knee contact is impossible.

The lower leg (and not the spurs) takes over as the main driving aid, since the seat cannot be used. If the lower leg slides back or starts to swing back and forth then the rider will lose balance. The foot is put slightly further into the stirrup with the ankle flexing so that the heel is the lowest part of the rider's body. Knee, lower leg, ankle and the foot in the stirrup make up the foundation. The foundation should always remain unaltered so that you build on it. In the forward seat, the shoulder, knee and heel forms a vertical line with the head in front of the vertical while the hips which are positioned further back at higher speeds act as a kind of pendulum, working with the lower leg to develop forwards impulsion.

Your head should be held naturally and just as in the dressage position you should look forwards between the horse's ears. When jumping a course you should look at the jumps and then look in the direction that you need to ride, turning the shoulder while keeping them parallel to your horse's. From relaxed shoulders the arms should be held in front of the body and the reins shortened so that the lower arm and reins form a straight line. The hands should be held on each side of the horse's neck in line about with the withers. Leg and hand aids are also applied independently of the movement of the rider's upper body.

The application of the aids from a forward seat is in principle the same as when in the dressage position. The seat aids are given from the knee and lower leg, since the seat itself is off the horse's back. To increase the tempo and extend the canter strides the lower leg is applied (with the upper body remaining still) so that the impulsion increases from the hindquarters. Turns are ridden through lesser or greater pressure being applied through the lower leg. It is important to watch that the outside rein dominates and is supported by the supporting outside leg. This will ensure that the horse doesn't fall out through the outside shoulder.

Note

The aids from the hand should be given independently from the seat in a forward position.

Shoulders, elbows and wrists need to stay relaxed, otherwise the body's movement will be transmitted through the hand and thus onto the horse. Naturally the horse should also be ridden on the bit when in a forward position, but not in the same outline as when riding dressage since at higher speeds and on uneven ground the horse needs to use his neck to balance himself.

Hacking out

When hacking out you should shorten your stirrups by at least two holes. To relieve your horse's back over long distances you should always trot rising and canter in a forward seat. The tempo will be quicker so it is much too tiring for both horse and rider for the rider to stay sitting in the saddle over longer stretches. The rider should always pay attention to where she is asking her horse to go, as even on familiar tracks or when going over stubble fields ridden many times before it is possible that a rabbit has been busy the night before. It is therefore important that the horse is always ridden on a contact so that you can react immediately to any threats or dangers.

Note

A rider has learned how to use the aids so they can be used at any time – especially when out hacking. You are responsible for your horse – and for the safety of others around you. It is irresponsible to act thoughtlessly or to tear around the countryside!

Riding up and down hill

The forward seat should always be used when riding up and down hill. The steeper the slope, the more out of the saddle and thus forward the rider should be. In all cases the horse should be ridden straight as long as he is not likely to lose his balance. Both lower legs should be on the horse to support him and ensure that he stays straight. The reins should be shortened with the hands moving forwards. If there is a longer

downhill stretch it is advisable to "bridge" the reins. To do this take a ten centimetre long section of rein above the grip of the right hand into the left so that a double section of rein is running between the hands. This bridge can be rested in front of the withers and used to support the rider and also guarantees that the hands stay quiet. This is important for the balance of both horse and rider.

Note

Steep gradients should always be ridden at a walk.

When the horse goes downhill he shortens up: his head will be close to the vertical and the hindquarters will reach forward underneath his

The horse shortens his body and his hind legs step under his centre of gravity. The rider shifts his weight back.

Here the horse is getting longer and pushes off with the hindquarters. The rider shifts his centre of gravity forwards.

centre of gravity. When riding uphill the horse gets longer: his head moves further forward and the hindquarters provide the impulsion.

Dealing with obstacles when out hacking

It is not only poles and jump stands, rocks or branches that form obstacles. A dry ditch, a shadowed puddle or a large grey rock on the edge of the path can all, under certain circumstances end what should be an enjoyable hack prematurely. In all situations it is vital that the rider stays calm.

If the rider sees an obstacle before her horse, she has the advantage. She has the chance to apply the seat and leg aids and to take up the reins so that there is a good contact. The voice can be used as well to ride quietly and firmly past, whatever""monster" is waiting. Since a horse can shy to the side at the last moment the contact with the saddle at the knee is vital. Once it is all over the horse should be praised. If a horse stops at a ditch or puddle give him plenty of time to look at it. The seat and legs should be clearly applied, as a movement to the

side or quickly swinging around should be avoided. Even if only step-by-step, he must move forwards!

It is more difficult if the rider is taken by surprise as well. Never daydream when out hacking; shrieking or shouting out a warning is also wrong! A horse's fear would only be reinforced and he would resort to his inbuilt instinct to run away. The rider needs to be in control of herself in order to convince her horse that there is nothing wrong and that "Wherever I go you go!". If a horse shies at a plastic bag in the hedge or wants to stay with his mates at the fence in the paddock next door, then you should turn him to the opposite side and ride him with the inside leg (i.e. the leg between the horse and the object), energetically passing the danger spot. Your voice should be used to calm and praise.

Keep calm and use the right aids.

31

Final comments

Now that you know how to apply the aids they shouldn't necessarily be viewed as "operating instructions for the horse". Horses don't unfortunately work like cars: engage the clutch, put into gear and accelerate. The rider's aids are normally all used together at once with the degree of each one varying. And each individual horse reacts differently. This is what makes learning to ride so challenging. Those who have a good seat will feel the aids working together quickest and easiest. If you know your horse and understand and love him as a horse, then you can develop this feeling and never risk over-facing him. If something goes wrong a rider should always look to herself first before punishing her horse. A rider needs much self control (not just bodily control) and patience to be able to get through thick and thin in harmony with her horse. Riders never stop learning!